ABRAHAM LINCOLN.

A

MEMORIAL DISCOURSE,

BY REV. T. M. EDDY, D. D.,

DELIVERED AT A

Union Meeting, held in the Presbyterian Church,

WAUKEGAN ILLINOIS,

WEDNESDAY, APRIL 19, 1865,

THE DAY UPON WHICH THE FUNERAL SERVICES OF THE PRESIDENT WERE CONDUCTED IN WASHINGTON, AND OBSERVED THROUGHOUT THE LOYAL STATES AS ONE OF MOURNING.

PUBLISHED BY REQUEST.

CHICAGO:
PRINTED AT THE METHODIST BOOK DEPOSITORY.

CHARLES PHILBRICK, PRINTER.
1865.

CORRESPONDENCE.

WAUKEGAN, APRIL 19, 1865.

REV. T. M. EDDY, D. D.:

The undersigned having listened with much interest and profit to your eloquent eulogy this day spoken before the citizens of this town, upon the Life and Death of President Lincoln, unite in requesting a copy for publication. We feel that much good would come to the community from a calm perusal of the thoughts so fitly uttered on the occasion.

H. W. BLODGETT,
C. W. UPTON,
W. J. LUCAS,
C. G. BUELL,
P. W. EDWARDS,
B. S. KENNICOTT,
S. S. GREENLEAF,
JOSEPH MALLON,
D. BREWSTER,
W. H. P. WRIGHT,
C. L. WRIGHT,
M. M. BIDDLECEW,
A. P. YARD,
WM. C. TIFFANY,
R. DOUGLAS,
JAMES Y. CORY.

EDITORIAL ROOMS, NORTHWESTERN CHRISTIAN ADVOCATE,
66 Washington Street, Chicago, April 24, 1865.

MESSRS. BLODGETT, UPTON AND OTHERS:

Gentlemen—Your note is before me. You know the time for the preparation of that discourse was very brief. You are also aware, doubtless, that though spoken from copious notes, much of it was extemporized, and that I cannot reproduce those passages. But such as it is, I place it in your hands, as my humble tribute to the name and the virtues of our murdered President.

With much respect, gentlemen,

Yours truly, T. M. EDDY.

MEMORIAL DISCOURSE.

"In the day of adversity consider."

It *is* the day of adversity. A great grief throws its shadow over heart and hearth and home. There is such a sorrow as this land never knew before; agony such as never until now wrung the heart of the nation. In mansion and cottage, alike, do the people bow themselves.

We have been through the Red Sea of war, and across the weary, desert marches of griefs and bereavements, but heretofore we have felt that *our leader* was with us, and believed that surely as Moses was led by the pillar of cloud and of fire, so did God lead him.

But now that leader is not. Slain, slain by the hand of the assassin, murdered beside his wife! The costliest blood has been shed, the clearest eye is closed, the strongest arm is nerveless—the Chief Magistrate is no more. "The mighty man cries bitterly; the day is a day of wrath, a day of trouble and distress, a day of wasteness and desolation, a day of darkness and gloominess, a day of clouds and thick darkness."

It is no mere official mourning which hangs its sad drapery everywhere. It is not alone that a President of the Republic is, for the first time, assassinated. No; there is the tender grief that characterizes the bereavement of a loved friend, which shows there was something in this man which grappled him to men's hearts as with hooks of steel.

But mourning the death of the Chief Magistrate, it becomes us to review the elements of his career as a ruler, which have so endeared him to loyal hearts.

If I were to sketch the model statesman, I would say he must have mental breadth and clearness, incorruptible integrity, strength of will, tireless patience, humanity, preserved from demoralizing weakness by conscientious reverence for law, ardent love of country, and, regulating all, a commanding sense of responsibility to God, the Judge of all. These, though wrapped in seeming rustic garb, were found in Abraham Lincoln. He had mental breadth and clearness. In spite of a defective early education, he became a self-taught thinker, and later in life he read widely and meditated profoundly, until he acquired a thorough mental discipline. He possessed the power to comprehend a subject at once in the aggregate and in its details. His eye swept a wide horizon and descried clearly all within its circumference. He was a keen logician, whose apt manner of "putting thin s" made him more than a match for practiced diplomatists and wily marplots. There were men of might about his council-board, scholars and statesmen, but none arose to his altitude, much less was either his master.

That very facetiousness sometimes critcised, kept him from becoming morbid, and gave healthfulness to his opinions, free alike from fever and paralysis. That his was incorruptible integrity, no man dare question. He was not merely above reproach, but eminently above suspicion. Purity is receptive. "Blessed are the pure in heart, for they shall *see God*," is as profound in philosophy as comprehensive in theology. Purity in the realm of moral decision and motive, is a skylight to the soul, through which truth comes direct. Abraham Lincoln was so pure in motive and purpose, looked so intensely after the right that he might pursue it, that he saw clearly where many walked in mist.

Without developing the characteristics of the ideal statesman analytically, let us see how they were manifest in his administration.

It began amid the rockings of rebellion. A servile predecessor, deplorably weak, if not criminal, had permitted treason to be freely mouthed in the national capitol, treasonable action to be taken by State authorities, and armed treason to resist and defy federal authority, and environ with bristling works the forts and flag of the Union. At such a juncture, Mr. Lincoln, then barely escaping assassination, was inaugurated. As was right, he made all proper efforts for conciliation, tendered the olive-branch, proposed such changes of existing laws, and even of the Constitution, as should secure Southern rights from the adverse legislation of a sectional majority. All was refused, and traitors said, "We will not live with you. Though you sign a blank sheet and leave us to fill it with our own conditions, we will not abide with you."

Refusing peace, war was commenced, not by the President, but by secessionists. War has been waged on a scale of astounding vastness for four years, and Mr. Lincoln falls as the day of victory dawns.

His claim to the character of a great statesman is to be estimated in view of the fiery ordeal which tried him, and not by the gauge of peaceful days. In addition to the most powerful armed rebellion ever organized, he was confronted by a skillful, able, persistent, well compacted partisan opposition. He was to harmonize sectional feelings as antagonistic as Massachusetts and Kentucky, and to rally to one flag generals as widely apart in sentiment and policy as Phelps and Fitz John Porter. That under such difficulties he sometimes erred in judgment and occasionally failed in execution, is not strange, for he was a man, but that he erred so seldom, and that he so admirably retrieved his mistakes, shows that he was more by far than an ordinary man; more by far than an average statesman. Standing where we do to-day, we feel that he was divinely appointed for the crisis; that he was chosen to be the Moses of our pilgrimage, albeit, he was to die at Pisgah and be buried against Beth-Peor, while a Joshua should be commissioned to lead us into the land of promise.

In studying the administration of these four eventful years, it seems to me there were four grand landmarks of principle governing him, ever visible to the eye of the President, by which he steadily made his way.

I. The Union is Incapable of Division.

In his first Inaugural he said: "I hold that in contemplation of universal law and of the Constitution, the Union of these States is perpetual." In his reply to Fernando Wood, then Mayor of New York, he said, "There is nothing that could ever bring me willingly to consent to the destruction of the Union." By this rule he walked. The Union was one for all time, and there was no authority for its division lodged anywhere. He would use no force, would exercise no authority not needed for this purpose. But what force *was* needed, whether moral or physical, should be employed. Hence the call for troops. Hence the marching armies of the Republic, and the thunder of cannon at the gates of Vicksburg, Charleston and Richmond. Hence the suspension of the *habeas corpus*, the seizure and occasional imprisonment of treason-shriekers and sympathizers, for which he has been denounced as a tyrant by journals, which, slandering him while living, have the effrontery to put on the semblance of grief and throw lying emblems of mourning to the wind! For the exercise of that authority, he went for trial to the American people, and they triumphantly sustained him.

II. The second grand regulating idea of his administration may be best stated in his own words: "GOVERNMENT OF THE PEOPLE BY THE PEOPLE, FOR THE PEOPLE." He conceded the people *to be the Government.* Their will was above the opinion of secretaries and generals. He recognized their right to dictate the policy of the administration. Their majesty was ever before him as an actual presence. On the 11th of February, 1861, he said, in Indianapolis, "Of the people when they rise in mass in behalf of the Union and the liberties of their country, it may be said, 'The gates of hell shall not prevail against them,'" and again, "I appeal to you to constantly bear in mind that with you, and not with politicians, not with the President, not with office-seekers, but *with you* rests the question, Shall the Union and shall the liberties of this country be preserved to the latest generation?" Again, on that memorable journey to Washington, he said, "It is with you, the people, to advance the great cause of the Union and the Constitution." "I am sure I bring a true heart to the work. For the ability to perform it, I must trust in that Supreme Being who has never forsaken this favored land, through the instrumentality of this great and intelligent people." In his first Inaugural he said: "This country, with its institutions, belongs to the people who inhabit it." "The Chief Magistrate derives all his authority from the people." "Why should there not be a patient confidence in the ultimate justice of the people? Is there any better or any equal hope in the world?"

These sentences were utterances of a faith within him. In the people he had faith. He saw them only lower than the King of kings, and they were to be trusted and obeyed.

Yet this man who thus trusted and honored the people, who so reverenced their authority, and bowed before their majesty, has been called "tyrant," "usurper," by men who now would make the world forget their infamy by putting on badges of woe, and who seek to wash out the record of their slander by such tears as crocodiles shed! Out upon the miserable dissemblers!

When the people had spoken, he bowed to their mandate. When it became necessary to anticipate their decision, he did so, calmly trusting their integrity and intelligence. He considered their wishes in the constitution of his cabinet, in the choice of military commanders, in the appointment of Chief Justice of the Supreme

Court of the United States, and in the measures he recommended to Congress.

The people proved worthy the trust. They promptly took every loan asked for the relief of the treasury and sustained the national credit. They answered all his calls for men. They sprang into the ranks, shouting

"We are coming, Father Abraham."

They cheerfully laid down life at his word. So far from this conflict proving a republic unfit to make war, or that for its prosecution there must be intensely centralized authority, it has demonstrated that a democracy trusted, is mightier than a dictatorship.

III. His third towering landmark was THE RIGHT OF ALL MEN TO FREEDOM. And here with his practical sense and acute vision he rose to a higher, and I think a healthier, elevation than that of many heroic anti-slavery leaders. They *were* anti-slavery. Their lives were spent in attack. They sought to destroy a system; they told its wrongs and categoried its iniquities.

He knew that light, let in, will cast out darkness, and that kindled warmth will drive out cold. He knew that freedom was better than slavery, and that when men see that it is so, they will decree freedom instead of slavery. He therefore entered the lists FOR FREEDOM. He spoke of its inestimable blessings, and then unrolling the immortal Declaration of Independence claimed that, with all its dignity and all its endowments, liberty is the birthright of ALL MEN. He taught the American people that the inalienable right of all men to liberty was the first utterance of the young Republic, and that her voice must be stifled so long as slavery lives. In his Ottawa speech he said: "Henry Clay—my beau-ideal of a statesman—the man for whom I fought all my humble life, once said of a class of men who would repress all tendencies to liberty and ultimate emancipation, that they must, if they would do this, go back to the era of our independence and muzzle the cannon which thunders its annual joyous return; they must blow out the moral lights around us, they must penetrate the human soul and eradicate there the love of liberty, and then, and not till then, could they perpetuate slavery in this country."

He laid his spear in rest and went forth with armor on, the champion of freedom. He claimed she should walk the world everywhere, untrammeled and free to bless the lowest as well as the highest. It was not right and never could be made right, to forbid working lawfully that all men might be free. Slavery debased—freedom lifted up. Slavery corrupted, freedom purified. Freedom might be abused, but slavery was itself a colossal abuse.

He was no dreaming visionary, but stated with commanding clearness the doctrine of equality before the law, or political equality, distinguishing it from social equality. In old Independence Hall, in 1861, he said of the Colonies: "I have often enquired of myself what great principle or idea it was that kept this confederacy so long together. It was not the mere matter of the separation of the Colonies from the mother land, but the sentiment in the Declaration of Independence which gave liberty, not alone to the people of this country, but I hope to the world for all future time. It was that which gave promise that in due time the weight should be lifted from the shoulders of all men." He held that instrument to teach that "nothing stamped with the Divine image and likeness was sent into the world to be trodden on, degraded and imbruted by its fellows."

We search vainly for a clearer and terser statement of the true theory of equality than he gave last autumn in an address to a Western regiment. "We have, as all will agree, a free government, where *every man has a right to be equal with every other man.*" Has a *right to be!* Take the fetters from his limbs, take the load of disability from his shoulders, give him room in the arena, and then if he cannot succeed with others, the failure is his. *But he has the right* TO TRY. You have no right to forbid the trial. If he will try for wealth, fame, political position, he has the right. Let him exercise it and enjoy what he lawfully wins.

With such views he came to the presidency. Here he was an executive officer, bound by the Constitution, and charged with its maintenance and defense. He was to take the nation as the people placed it in his hands, rule it under the Constitution and surrender it unbroken to his successor. Accordingly he made to the Southern States all conceivable propositions for peace. Slavery should be left without federal interference. They madly rejected all. War came. He saw at the outset that slavery was our bane. It confronted each regiment, perplexed each commander. It was the Southern commissariat, dug Southern trenches and piled Southern breastworks.

But certain Border States maintained a quasi loyalty and clung to slavery. They were in sympathy with rebellion, but wore the semblance of allegiance and with consequential airs assumed to dictate the policy of the President. He was greatly embarrassed. He made them every kind and conciliatory offer, but all was refused. Slavery on the gulf and on the border, in Charleston and in Louisville, was the same intolerant, incurable enemy of the Union. He struck it at last. The Proclamation of Emancipation came, followed in due time by the recommendation that the Constitution be so amended as forever to render slavery impossible in State or Territory. For these acts he was arraigned before the American people on the 8th of last November, and received their emphatic approval.

In a letter written to a citizen of Kentucky, the President gave an exposition of his policy so transparent, that I reproduce it in this place. It is his sufficient explanation and vindication.

"EXECUTIVE MANSION, WASHINGTON,
"April 4, 1864.

A. G. HODGES, ESQ., Frankfort, Ky.

"*My Dear Sir:*—You ask me to put in writing the substance of what I verbally stated the other day, in your presence, to Governor Bramlette and Senator Dixon. It was about as follows:

"I am naturally anti-slavery. If slavery is not wrong nothing is wrong. I cannot remember when I did not so think and feel; and yet I have never understood that the Presidency conferred upon me an unrestricted right to act officially in this judgment and feeling. It was in the oath I took that I would to the best of my ability preserve, protect and defend the Constitution of the United States. I could not take the office without taking the oath. Nor was it in my view that I might take the oath to get power, and break the oath in using the power. I understood, too, that in ordinary civil administration this oath even forbade me to practically indulge my primary abstract judgment on the moral question of slavery. I had publicly declared this many times and in many ways; and I aver that, to this day, I have done no official act in mere deference to my abstract judgment and feeling on slavery. I did understand, however, that my oath to preserve the Constitution to the best of my ability imposed upon me the duty of preserving, by every indispensable means, that government, that nation, of which that Constitution was the organic law. Was it possible to lose the nation, and yet preserve the Constitution? By general law, life *and* limb must be protected; yet often a limb must be amputated to save a life, but a life is never wisely given to save a limb. I felt that measures, otherwise unconstitutional, might become lawful by becoming indispensable to the preservation of the Constitution through the preservation of the nation. Right or wrong, I assumed this ground, and now avow it. I could not feel that to the best of my ability I had even tried to preserve the Constitution, if, to save slavery, or any minor matter, I should permit the wreck of government, country, and Constitution altogether. When, early in the war, General Fremont attempted military emancipation, I forbade it, because I did not then think it an indispensable necessity. When, a little later, General Cameron, then Secretary of War, suggested the arming of the blacks, I objected, because I did not yet think it an indispensable necessity. When, still later, General Hunter attempted military emancipation, I forbade it, because I did not yet think the indispensable necessity had come. When, in March and May and July, 1862, I made earnest and successive appeals to the Border States to favor compensated emancipation, I believed the indispensable necessity for military emancipation and arming the blacks would come, unless averted by that measure. They declined the proposition; and I was, in my best judgment, driven to the alternative of either surrendering the Union, and with it the Constitution, or of laying strong hand upon the colored element. I chose the latter. In choosing it, I hoped for greater gain than loss; but of this I was not entirely confident. More than a year of trial now shows no loss by it in our foreign relations, none in our home popular sentiment, none in our white military force—no loss by it anyhow or anywhere. On the contrary, it shows a gain of quite a hundred and thirty thousand soldiers, seamen, and laborers. These are palpable facts, about which, as facts, there can be no caviling. We have the men; and we could not have had them without the measure.

"And now let any Union man who complains of the measure test himself by writing down in one line that he is for subduing the rebellion by force of arms; and in the next, that he is for taking three [one?] hundred and thirty thousand men from the Union side, and placing them where they would be but for the measure he condemns. If he cannot face his case so stated, it is only because he cannot face the truth.

"I add a word which was not in the verbal conversation. In telling this tale, I attempt no compliment to my own sagacity. I claim not to have controlled events, but confess plainly that events have controlled me. Now, at the end of three years' struggle, the nation's condition is not what either party or any man desired or expected. God alone can claim it. Whither it is tending seems plain. If God now wills the removal of a great wrong, and wills also that we of the North, as well as you of the South, shall pay fairly for our complicity in that wrong, impartial history will find therein new causes to attest and revere the justice and goodness of God.

"Yours truly, A. LINCOLN."

He struck slavery because slavery had clutched the throat of the Republic, and one of the twain must die! Mr. Lincoln said, LET IT BE SLAVERY!

Christianity, declaring the brotherhood of race, redemption and retribution answered, *So be it!* The Bible, sealed by slave-codes to four millions for whom its truths were designed, answered *Amen!* The gospel long fettered by the slave-master's will, and instead of an evangel of freedom made to proclaim a message of bondage, lifted up its voice in thanksgiving. Marriage, long dishonored, put on its robes of purity, and its ring of perpetual covenant, and answered *Amen*, and from above, God's strong angels and six-winged cherubim, bending earthward, shouted their response to the edict of the Great Emancipator!

IV. The next controlling idea was

PROFOUND RELIGIOUS DEPENDENCE.

As a public man, he set God before his eyes, and did reverence to the Most High. It was deeply a touching scene as he stood upon the platform of the car which was to carry him from his Springfield home, and tearfully asked his neighbors and old friends that they should remember him in their prayers. Amid tears and sobs they answered "We will pray for you." Again and again has he publicly invoked Divine aid, and asked to be remembered in the prayers of the people. His second Inaugural seems rather the tender pastoral of a white-haired bishop than a political manifesto.

What were his personal relations to his God, I know not. We are not in all things able to judge him by our personal standard. How much etiquette may have demanded, how much may have been yielded to the tyranny of custom we cannot tell. In public life he was spotless in integrity and dependent upon Divine aid. He had made no public consecration to God in church covenant, but we may not enter the sanctuary of his inner life. He constantly read the holy oracles, and recognized their claim to be the inspired Scriptures.

He felt that religious responsibility when he sent forth the Proclamation of Emancipation closing with this sublime sentence: "And upon this act, sincerely believed to be an act of justice, warranted by the Constitution, on military necessity, I invoke the considerate judgment of mankind and the gracious favor of Almighty God."

In one of the gloomy hours of the struggle he said to a delegation of clergymen: "My hope of success in this great and terrible struggle rests on that immutable foundation, the justice and goodness of God. And when events are very threatening, and prospects very dark, I still hope, in some way which men cannot see, all will be well in the end, because our cause is just and God is on our side."

If, as the executive officer of the nation he erred, it

was in excessive tenderness in dealing with criminals. Unsuspecting and pure, he could not credit unmixed guilt in others, and with difficulty could he bring himself to suffer condign punishment to be inflicted. There were times when he was inflexible. In vain did wealth and position plead for Gardner, the slave-captain. As vainly did they for Beall and Johnson. If he was lenient it was the error of amiableness.

In reviewing the administration of Abraham Lincoln, we see in him another of those Providentially called and directed leaders who have been raised up in great crises. His name stands on the roll with those of Moses and Joshua, and William of Orange, and Washington. Not only did Providence raise him up, but it divinely vindicated his dealings with slavery. As emancipation was honored, did the pillar of flame light our hosts on to victory!

In the dawning morn of peace and Union has this leader been slain. When the nation thought it most needed him, has he been basely butchered! As the ship which had been rocking in the waves and bowing before the storm was reaching the harbor, a pirate, who sailed with the passengers, basely stole on deck and shot the pilot at the wheel!

The assassin has been held in abhorrence among all people and in all ages. Here was a foul plot to destroy at one swoop the President, the officers eligible to the succession, the Cabinet, the Lieutenant-General, and no doubt the loyal Governors of the States. That the scheme was successful only in part, God be praised.

Never has an assassination produced so terrible a shock. For—

> "He had borne his faculties so meek, had been
> So clear in his great office, that his virtues
> Do plead like angels, trumpet-tongued, against
> The deep damnation of his taking off."

He fell, and the whole land mourns. Secession smote him in her impotent death-rage, but the State lives on! The reins which dropped from his nerveless hand another grasped, and the nation lives. No revolution comes. No war of rival dynasties! The constitutional successor is in the chief seat of power, and how much secession has taken by this new crime remains to be seen.

Fellow-citizens, there are some duties which press upon us in this hour.

1. We must anew commit ourselves to the work of suppressing rebellion and re-enthroning the majesty of the Union and Constitution. Mr. Lincoln lived until the nation's flag had waved in triumph over every important Southern city; until the proud Southern aristocracy had thrown itself at the feet of its slaves, and with frantic outcries implored salvation at their hands; had lived to walk through Richmond, and be hailed by its dusky freedmen as their deliverer; had lived until he received the report of the surrender of Lee's grand army, and then he was slain. We must complete the work. Onward, until it be wrought. We believe it will be soon, but were it a hundred years it must be accomplished!

2. We must complete the destruction of slavery. Added to its long catalogue of crimes, it has now slain the Lord's Anointed, the man whom he made strong! Now as THE ETERNAL liveth, it must die! By the

agonies it has caused, by the uncoffined graves it has filled, by the tears it has wrung from pure women and little children, by our sons and brothers starved to death in its mined prisons, by our beloved Chief Magistrate murdered, by all these do we this day swear unto the LORD that slavery SHALL DIE, and that he who would save it shall politically die with it!

3. This day, as funeral rites are being said, and sobs are coming up from a smitten household and bereaved people, before the Lord do we solemnly demand that justice be done in the land upon evil-doers, that blood-guiltiness may be taken away, and that men shall not dare repeat such crimes.

When treason slew Abraham Lincoln, it slew the pardoning power, and by its own act placed authority in the hands of one of sterner mold and fiery soul—one deeply wronged by its atrocities. Now let it receive the reward of its own hands! This is the demand of mercy as well as justice, that after generations may see the expiation of treason is too costly for its commission. Mercy to the many demands the punishment of the guilty.

The assassin of the Chief Magistrate must be found. Though all seas must be crossed, all mountains ascended, all valleys traversed, he *must* be found! If he hide him under the mane of the British lion, beneath the paw of the Russian bear or among the lilies of France, he must be found and plucked thence for punishment! If there be no extradition treaty, then the strong hands of our power must make one. He was a tragedian. Had he never read—

> "If the assassination
> Could trammel up the consequences and catch

With this surcease, success; that but this blow
Might be the be-all and the end-all *here*,
* * * * * *
"We'd jump the life to come. But in these cases
We still have judgment here. We but teach
Bloody inventions, which, being taught, return
To plague the inventors. Thus even-handed justice
Commends the ingredients of our poisoned chalice
To our own lips."

We are told that he excelled in the part of Richard III. Did he not remember the tent scene—

"My conscience hath a thousand several tongues,
And every tongue brings in a several tale,
And every tale condemns me for a villain—
Perjury, perjury, in the highest degree,
Murder, stern murder, in the darkest degree;
All several sins, all used in each degree,
Throng to the bar, crying all—Guilty! guilty!
I shall despair. There is no creature loves me;
And, if I die, no soul will pity me."

He has murdered the Lord's Anointed, and vengeance shall pursue him. Tell me not, in deprecation of this sentiment "Vengeance is mine, I will repay saith the Lord." Human justice has its work and must follow the assassin, if need be, to the very gates of hell! It is God's edict that he who causelessly takes any human life, "By men shall his blood be shed"—how much more when it is such a life!*

A morning journal, which has been somehow retained in the interest of wrong, of home-traitors, of misrule, has already impliedly put in the plea of insanity for the

---

* Since the MS. of this discourse was given the printer, the assassin has met his retribution. Hunted like a wild beast to his lair, he was surrounded by his pursuers, forsaken by his accomplice, the barn to which he had fled fired, then shot to death, lingering several hours in intense suffering and his remains consigned to impenetrable obscurity. Retribution came to him before his victim was buried. So be it ever! His accomplices are known and *must be* punished.

assassin. The same journal runs a parallel between him and John Brown. Well, Virginia executed John Brown —its own precedent is fatal to its own client!

Let justice be done on the leaders of rebellion. Have done with the miserable cant of curing those perjured conspirators with kindness. Libby Prison mined under Federal captives, the starved skeletons of our slowly murdered kinsmen, the grave of Lincoln, and the gaping wounds of Seward are your answer. It must be taught men for all time that treason is, in this life, unpardonable! It is all crimes in one. In this case it is without the glitter of seeming chivalry for its relief. It has had nothing knightly. It has conspired to starve prisoners, has plotted conflagrations which were to consume, in one dread holocaust, the venerable matron, the gray-haired sire and the mother with her babe; has resorted to poison, the knife of the cut-throat and the pistol of the assassin. No treason was ever so repulsively foul, so reekingly corrupt. For its great leaders, the block and the halter; for its chieftains, military and civic, of the second class, perpetual banishment with confiscation of their goods, for all who have volunteered to fight against the Union perpetual disfranchisement—these are the demands of a long-suffering people.

The case of treason-sympathizers among us is one of grave moment. It is hard to bear their sneers and patiently to listen to their covert treason. It is a question whether the limit of toleration has not been passed. The era of assassination has been commenced. Be sure that any man who will excuse an assassin, will himself do foul murder when he can shoot from behind a hedge, or strike a victim in the back. It is matter of self-defence to cast such from our midst. Let us have no violence, no lawlessness, *but such persons must be persuaded to depart from us.* "They are gentlemen." Booth was courtly in speech and mien. Have they been State officers? So has Walsh, whose house was a disunion arsenal. The time has come when we cannot permit men in sympathy with armed rebellion, which employs the assassin, to dwell in our midst.

Abraham Lincoln is no more. His work is done. We may not comprehend the mystery which permitted his removal at such an hour, in such a way. God hideth himself wondrously, and sometimes seems to stand afar from His truth and His cause when most needed.

Our leader is gone. His work is finished, and it may be that his Providential mission was fully accomplished. His memory is imperishably fragrant. WASHINGTON—LINCOLN! Who shall say which name shall shine brighter in the firmament of the historic future!

He is dead! In the Presidential Mansion are being said words of solemn admonition and godly counsel. In a few hours his remains will be on their way to sleep in their Illinois grave!

Dead! "How is the strong staff broken and the beautiful rod!"

Pray devoutly for the smitten widow and fatherless children of our Chief Magistrate. They are sorely stricken and God alone can heal them. To them it is not the loss of the Chief Magistrate that makes this hour so sad, but that they have no more a husband or a father!

And now that there has been sorrow in all the land, and the death-angel in all its homes, from the humblest to the highest, is not our expiation well-nigh wrought, and will not our Father have compassion upon us?

Let us devoutly pray the King of nations to guide *our nation* through its remaining struggle! It may be He means to show us that He alone is the Savior!

Let us implore Divine guidance upon Mr. Lincoln's successor, Andrew Johnson, President of the United States. He was faithful amid the faithless. He was true to the Union when few in his section had for it aught but curses. Pray for him. He comes to power at a critical time and needs wisdom from above. Confide in him. He will surely rise above the one error which temporarily drew him down. He is only hated by traitors, and when they hate, it is safe for loyal men to trust.

By and by we may understand all this. Now it passes comprehension, but we have seen so many manifestations of God's supervising agency when we least looked for it, that we may safely trust Him. He means to save us. Nay, blessed be His name, He *has* saved us!

His grand purposes will go forward. The wrath of man shall praise Him, and the remainder of wrath will He restrain. Remember, and take heart as you remember, the ringing line of Whittier.

"God's errands never fail."

He who rides upon the whirlwind and directs the storm, is neither dead nor sleeping, and He is a God who never compromises with wrong, and never abdicates His throne.

www.ingramcontent.com/pod-product-compliance
Lightning Source LLC
LaVergne TN
LVHW011142110826
845150LV00008B/2475

* 9 7 8 1 4 1 8 1 9 1 9 4 8 *